I0847388

not fine

Kerry Love

For my mother, Kathleen,
who taught me the words
and to love them

Ippy - oy - add

Somtimes I'm mad
Othertimes I'm glad
But often I feel Ippy - oy - add
Which is......
A teaspoon of sad
A pinch of mad
Two cups full of joy
A spoonful of toys
A whole quart of daffy
And a half gallon happy
Add I almost forgot a carton of glad
And thats how I feel

IPPY-OY-ADD

By: Kerry Spengler

Ippy-Oy-Ad

Sometimes I'm mad
Other times I'm glad
But often I feel Ippy-oy-add
Which is…
A teaspoon of sad
A pinch of mad
Two cups full of joy
A spoonful of toys
A whole quart of daffy
And a half gallon happy
And I almost forgot a carton of glad
And that's how I feel
IPPY-OY-ADD

Kerry (Age 9)

ACKNOWLEDGMENTS

Special thanks to Jill Houston. Best friend? Confidant? Therapist? Soulmate? After all this time together, there are still no words. You are the greatest gift.

To Carrie Adams—my friend, my editor. Thank you for believing in me.

To my friends and family who gave me such lovely feedback on this journey especially Alicia Welch, Jeff Buenz, Genna Rose, Desi Draws, Ali Ferguson, Chris Denu, Kristopher Houston, Gretchen Klayman, Paula Williams, Alice Getchell, Ann Mulcahy, Mary Jane Walton, and Jim Gibbons.

To my Charleston crew, the amazing women who helped me find my wings, I will be forever grateful.

All of your love and support have meant the world to me. A thousand thank yous and many lifetimes of love. Always.

CONTENTS

CONTENTS

CHOICE

Psst
You do not get a prize
For knowing the most
For being well-informed
For having an opinion
There is no award
For worrying
Or overthinking
For analyzing
Or tearing a thing (yourself included) apart
There is no trophy
For being sensible
No ribbon for hoping least
Or being most realistic
Nothing will save you
From death or a broken heart
The choice is only
In how you meet them

WATER

Prayer For Today

Though the water seems still
May I trust
That so much has already changed
Just below the surface

A DROP

You told me once that
It only takes a single drop
To make water flow
A question
A butterfly
A glance
A sunset
And I am drowning

HOPE

I have been here
Long enough
To know
A promise is a wish
And forever is a maybe
But I do want to ask you
One thing
My lover
Do you hope
That it is me
In the end

NO MISTAKES

I hung up before you answered
But what I wanted to say was
I miss you I still love you there is no one else there never could be
anyone else it's only you now and forever
And
I will wait until you see it too because there is no other heartbeat I
feel pulsing through my fingers but yours
And
You inspire me to dance write sing everything
And
My soul will accept nothing less than you
And me
"You call me?"
Yeah, I guess I did.

When you are sad

It feels like gravity

Is suddenly stronger

The weight tugging

My heart down

Turning it into

A keyhole

For your sorrow

To slip through

And make its way out

Though my eyes

GRAVITY

MATTER

Licentiously
Is what you texted me
Out of the blue
And I thought, just maybe, you had read it,
Looked it up,
Savored its meaning
The precise way I savor
Butter, dripping down my chin
Chocolate, smeared across my lips
Champagne, dancing on my tongue
And words.
Like they matter.
Because they always have.
Words
Are the key to
Everything.
And I thought, just maybe, you really knew me
I wonder now if you were calling me a whore
Pretentiously.
In which case,
The words still mattered.

CHANGE

A drunk girl is not
Spare change
Abandoned by a hurried
Or careless stranger
She is not yours to pick up
And put in your pocket
She is not fair game
Free money
To be spent however you please
If you disagree
And somehow think you have a right
To her humanity
Because she has for a moment
Stopped guarding it with her life
(Because it is exhausting for women
To have to constantly defend
Our own humanity)
If you doubt that it still belongs to her
And see fit to take it
I can tell you
The price you pay for her humanity
Is the complete destruction
Of your own

STRONGER

Your chain

Around my ankle

Didn't keep me

From flying

It only made my wings

Stronger

When you think
Of me
A seed is planted
In my heart
That is tended with
Every beat, every pulse
Until life is squeezed from the shell
I can feel the intoxicating pain
Of new growth
The vine sprouting
Between my shoulders
Tickling the back of my neck
Placing a kiss just below my ear
Whispering
Of intimacies yet to be
Blooming in my mind
Until I believe
That it was me
Who was thinking
Of you

SEED

This feels like home
You said to me
After we danced and sang
All night long
Between the red rocks
Under a full moon
Among the deer who didn't run
But sauntered across our path
After you held my hand in yours
Against your chest
Connected
Like we had been our whole life
Because we have
And maybe even before

HOMESICK

This feels like home
You said to me
After you played me
The song about the fallen king
Kneeling before his Queen B
That made me cry
Before you knelt before me
And called me
Your queen
Long after I fell in love with you
But before I could admit it

This feels like home
You said to me
Before you left
For some place else
Before you left me
Homesick

FORGIVE
ME

The pain we pulled
From the deep wounds
Of each other
Breaks my heart
When I think of it
Wishing I hadn't hurt you
Wishing I hadn't hurt me
Forgive me
Forgive me
Forgive me
Our soul whispers

GROWING

That pain you feel

Is not your heart

Breaking

It is your heart

Growing

Large enough

To love yourself

Through something

You never thought you could

Survive

QUIETLY

Come lover
Let's be ordinary
Let's hold hands and talk and fall asleep in each
other's arms
I'll make you think and you'll make me laugh and
we'll dance in the kitchen to Lionel Richie
And every morning before you wake, I'll kiss your
forehead
And every night before you sleep, I'll kiss your lips
We'll take walks and watch movies and read to each
other in bed
Come lover, let's be ordinary
While we quietly change the world

Come lover
Let's be extraordinary
Let's help people and write things that make them feel
and travel the globe
I'll make you proud and you'll make me better and
we'll dance on the beach in the south of France
And every morning before you wake, I'll kiss your
forehead
And every night before you sleep, I'll kiss your lips
We'll take journeys and watch sunsets and keep each
other grounded as we soar
Come lover, let's be extraordinary
While we quietly change the world

HOLD ME

I am happy
To do most anything
Alone
But this body
Cannot hold me
By herself
Much longer

MOSAIC

Sometimes when I stretch
Pieces of you
Fall out
Glittery glass
Bright and sharp
That cause tiny
Explosions
Of tears
I guess we all
Carry with us
Shards of
Broken words
Broken hearts
Broken dreams
And can either
Leave them scattered
Or gather them
And make ourselves
Whole

If I could rewrite
The letter I sent
(And my life)
I would remove the insult of cliché
With care
Like a stain from lace
I would add an I'm sorry
Or maybe two
And a thousand more
I love yous

EDITS

TIDES

We have been playing
Like children in the sand
Building castles
With higher walls
And deeper moats
Foolishly
Arming ourselves
Against each other
Instead of
The oncoming tides

Where do all the words go?
The ones you never say to me
Do they go scurrying away
Under the light
Like some nocturnal creature
Hiding in your mind
Or maybe they get
Stuck between
Your heart and your throat
Making a knot so big
You cannot speak
Is there an I'm sorry
Tucked behind your ear
Hiding from your mouth
An I love you
Wedged between your ribs
Piercing you a little
Each time you breathe
Is there a hello
I miss you
I want you
Stuffed in your pocket forgotten
Only to disintegrate
In the wash
Where do all the words go?
The ones you never say to me
The ones that cast the spell
Setting me free
To love you
To forgive you
To let you go

SILENCE

PAPER SHIPS

I have
Been
Sending you
My love
On tiny
Paper ships
One word at a time
Across a sea of silence
Without knowing
If they ever make it
Safely to your shore
This must be what they mean
When they say faith is hard

When I remember

How you sent me

Words

Like they were flowers

Plucked from

The magnificent garden

Of your heart

I remember us

And let everything

That isn't

Go

PLUCK

I have come
To love
The sweet way
My tears
Tickle my skin
As they slide down
The side of
My face

HEALING

FORGIVENESS

A thank you
To someone who
Hurt you
Is a beautiful substitute
For an apology
You never got

AIR

Prayer For Today

I am sorry
For every moment
I haven't loved being me
For wasting time
Trying to be anything else
For insulting god

I ran from longing
And hid behind
A wall
I punished longing
And tried to
Banish her
I denied longing
And pretended
She was gone
I sat with longing
Held her close
And found you
Under a shady
Tree
Waiting for me

FOUND

You
You there
Crying

THERE

Feeling like you failed
At doing or being or loving
You there
You are so beautifully human
So
Beautifully
Human

SUMMER OF LOVE

It's 1967 you said to me
In a dream
That summer
In my arms
There are no coincidences
I thought and put it
In the pocket of my mind
Where it stayed until yesterday
When I turned the corner
Of Nowhere and Whatsnext
To find that 1967 was
The Summer of Love
A break from what was
To Imagine
What could be

EVERYTHING

I am fine, she says
And means it
She has healed
A thousand cuts
A hundred breaks
A dozen gaping wounds
She is a warrior
She is fine

Until the spiral
Knocks her to her knees
Again
Pierces her heart
Steals her breath
She has survived so much
But still breaks
At a loss so tiny
It is everything

WONDER

If you should ever wonder
Sitting in traffic
Or tossing in bed
On a night when the moon is full
And you can't sleep
If on your run one day
My words cross your mind
As you cross the street
Making your way home
If you feel a pang
Some hopeless Sunday
When you hear that song
We danced to the night under the stars
If on the perfect spring day
You roll down your window
And the scent of my perfume
Like fresh flowers and a smile
Finds you on the breeze
If you should ever wonder
Whether I still love you
I do

NAKED

I stood

Naked

Before you

With my scars

Under a spotlight

For your inspection

Forgetting that

I am worthy

Forgetting

Who I am

Wondering why

You ran

SURRENDER

Certainty
Visits me
On the wings of a crow
And leaves me
Just the
Same

I don't know if
I gave up
Or I became free
Or if those are
Just the
Same

GRACE

I have always been a bigot
But no one minds
My prejudice
For the white man
Who abandoned me
Leaving room for another
To creep into my crib
And steal the womb
From the mother I will never be
Making space for the
Ones who came after
To colonize me
With their pain
Robbing me of
Strength
Dignity
Choice
These things may make
My bigotry seem fair
But it is no longer
Fair to me
How can I heal
How can they heal
If I cannot forgive
Where will the grace
Come from?
In the asking
It appears

HERE

I don't wish you the stroke. But I wish you the grace from the stroke.
- Baba Ram Dass

These words ran through
The center of my heart
The way the block ran through
The center of my brain
And broke it wide open
Just the same
While my tears whispered
Here is the grace
Privileged white male
Embodies love
Show me the way home

I DO

I am no longer
The person you met
Under the sunset
On the solstice
I look a little like her
But I assure you
She is gone
I think you will
Like this woman
Better
And even if you don't
I do

ALL

I have no man
I have no home
I have no child
To call my own
But I have these words
And don't you see
That's all the woman
I need to be

The ego is not
An opponent
To be beaten into submission
The ego is a child
Soothed into calm
Through love
And when she is
Sneaky or
Mean or
Spiteful
You must try and
Love her more
People are
The same

THE
SAME

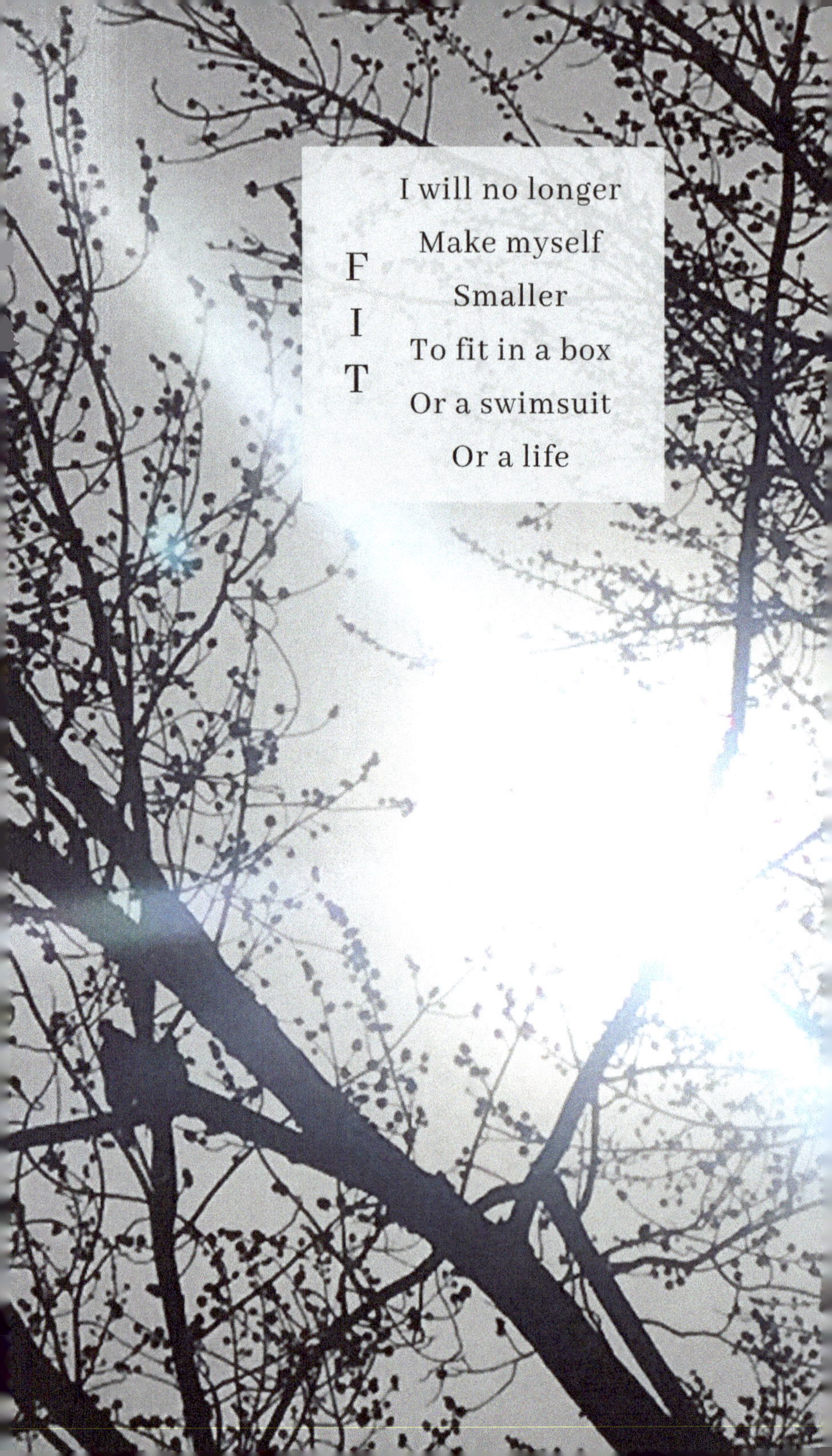

F I T

I will no longer
Make myself
Smaller
To fit in a box
Or a swimsuit
Or a life

For so many years
My body has held
My secrets

THIS
BODY

Like a faithful horse
Pulling a wagon
For the settler
Never settled
When I finally stopped to ask
What she was holding
For her seams were bursting
No longer able to contain me
She slowly laid out
My wares
And we decided together to discard them
Until we got to the
Heavy black trunk
At the back of my mind
Before I was ready
But much later than she needed me to be
We opened that trunk
Filled with so much darkness
And together we
Unloaded as much of it
As we could
I know there were pieces
She slipped out
And discarded
Before I could see
The horror they contained
Memories faded
Like bruises
How merciful
This body of mine

I have hair on my butt
And on my upper lip.
I shave it to maintain the illusion.
But even shaving doesn't help
When I miss the same twelve hairs on my ankle
For weeks at a time.
My hands are crepe-y
Too wrinkled for someone my age
I like to think they hold the lines of
All of the lives I've had.
Sometimes my breath smells
Like a T-rex has pooped in my mouth.
My dog farts.
I probably do, too.
I blow my nose like a truck driver.
My mother told me so but I never really believed
Until I heard it this summer at the truck stop.
I enjoy eating so much
That I dance a jig in anticipation
Of the meatball or the donut.
I am a terrible hostess.
Happy like a dog to greet my guests
But forgetting always to offer them
A drink
A snack
A seat.

PERFECT

My feet are too small for my body.
Sometimes I fall over.
I say fuck way too much for any sane person.
And if you were to tap my vein,
Like you might tap a maple tree,
You will likely find the same thing in both.
Sugar.
I get it wrong
Probably more than I get it right.
Yet I know
That I am
Perfect for you

DANCE

I wept when I met
My body again
It had been so long
Since she had
Been mine
It took years before
I could finally
Allow her
To be played
By the music

You must tell the world
Who you are
If you are waiting
For another
To define
To agree
To sanction
You have already
Forgotten

You must claim
Your power
If you are waiting
For time
For proof
For permission
You have already
Lost

You must love yourself
Exactly as you are
If you are waiting
For wisdom
For beauty
For perfection
You have already
Failed

MUST

You must create
The life you deserve
If you are waiting
For later
For more
For a savior
You have already
Died

You must imagine
The world we need
If you are waiting
For direction
For guidance
For others
There will never be
Change

FLY

Don't jinx them you said
And it became clear
How you viewed me
And probably all women
Like we're dangerous
Ready to bewitch you
At any moment
Ready to take away your freedom
But look closer my darling
I'm not your cage
I am your wings

PRIZE

It occurs to me
When I think of
Reaching out for you
That the prize
Does not reach out to the boxer
She does not climb into the ring behind him
And beg him to want her
So when you are ready
To finally win
Put down your fists
And come
Find me

I am too much
I'm not impressed by
Your job or your fancy car
I don't care where you've been
Only where you are
I don't want jewels
Or to take all your time
I'm not interested in
Your perfect body
Or what you think of mine

I am too much
I will see all of you
Not just what you show
It will make you feel naked
To realize I know
What you hide from the world
What you think no one saw
You will run from me
When it makes you feel raw

I am too much
Though I splash in shallows
I dwell in depths
Because I am the mirror
To what you forget
I can't help but reflect
All of your sides
You'll blame me when you see
The parts you don't like

TOO MUCH

I am too much
Because I am not here
To wear masks or play games
One gaze from my soul
Will set yours into flames
And make you face
What you'd rather ignore
I see you, I know you
And still love you more
I am too much

I will bring forth
The child in you
And the wise old soul
And with my brilliant heart
I will shine on them both
And see you how you have
Never been seen
And love you how you have
Never been loved
And it will all feel like
Too much

Because I am too much
But what if
No one else
Will ever be enough

ADORED

It feels like I have been waiting
For you
All day
Forever
To come pluck me
From the garden
Of my thoughts
And hold me
To your face
Inhale me
Allow me to brighten
Your world
Does a flower
Never adored
Ever fully bloom?

RESPECT

It was

Amazing

Loving you

I will not

Disrespect

My heart

By

Regretting it

NOT FINE

I am not fine
That even food gives me
No pleasure anymore
And admitting that
I was not fine
Made me burst
Into hysterics
The likes I haven't seen
Since my soul dumped me
And I found out
What she was hiding

I am not fine
That a baby would never stay
In the cage of my wounded body
While this country
Keeps other people's babies in cages
I'm not fine
That I've never even felt safe enough
In this world
To truly want to bring a baby here
Because all babies are
Our babies
And we're not keeping them safe
Because we weren't kept safe
None of us

I am not fine
That I am mad at men
But I can see that the system
That is poisoning all of us
May be poisoning them
The most
Because they cannot call their friends
When they are sobbing
As they transcend their pain
There can be no witness
They cannot ask to be held by someone that
They do not want to fuck
So they are not just broken
They are broken and alone
So I can't be mad at men
But I am

I am not fine
That I want a man
And I don't want a man
And that all of them leave me
I'm not fine
Spending every day
Trying to figure out
How to just love myself more
And then maybe one of them
Could love me enough
To stay
(It feels like a trap)

I am not fine
That the only sex that
Gives me pleasure is
Alone
And afterwards I cry
Alone

I am so not fine
That writing this is
Giving me a panic attack
And my lungs are burning
From the smoke
That blankets my state
In this land on fire
I can't breathe
I. Can't. Breathe.
Is what he said
I can't breathe

I am not fine
That everything is sponsored
And even super heroes
Wear capes covered in logos
Caught in the web
Of greed that feeds itself
But maybe they always have
After all what is a logo
In a world named by men
Who have tried to own it

I am not fine
That the Christians don't listen
To what Christ said
But instead to the churches
They make their checks out to
And the voters don't listen
To the words directly from the source
But drink the spin that profits
From making everything worse

I am not fine
That I live in an age
Where all the literature
In the world
Is in my hand
And I can only focus
Long enough to read
A meme

I am not fine
That my number one
Is a dog
Who has trouble getting up stairs
And I'm afraid if I lose him
I will be utterly
Lost

I am not fine
That I cannot find
The balance between wanting more
And wanting less
And I am afraid
I've exchanged creature comforts
And freedom
For love and respect
But shouldn't relationships
Have them all?

I am not fine
That my brother has lost
His job and his unborn baby
And his wife but when I ask him
He says he is fine
I am not fine
That I cannot shake him and say
"Wake up
Wake up
Wake up
You are not fine
You cannot look away from your phone
For a moment
Except to drink or drug
Or busy
Your way
Out of yourself"

I am not fine
That this world is so thick
With hunger and fear
That just cleaning my toilet
Feels like an accomplishment
When I walk around
With thousands of symphonies
In my heart
That I do not know
How to get out

I am not fine
That I cannot heal people
Who are hurting
But I cannot carry it
For them anymore

I am not fine
That I don't know how to help people
So I only sometimes
Try to

I am not fine
That I am unsure about everything
But as a teacher
I still have to
Give a grade

I am not fine that
I hear warring demons
Every time I think of sharing myself
One saying "you just want attention"
The other saying "it might help someone"
And I'm not fine
That I care so much about
Which one of them is right
(Both)

I am not fine
That I hear this poem
Out loud in my head
But I don't know if I will ever
Have the courage to
Say it out loud
And share it
And not have people like it
Because it is so much of me
And I'm not fine
That at 43 that still makes me scared

I am not fine
That I live in a country
That gives white men
All the power
To love this world
But they only want to win it

I am not fine
That my heart hurts so badly
All the time
While some people's hearts
Don't seem to work at all
But my god tells me to
Love them anyway

I am not fine
That I still care about being pretty
Even though I know
It's what's on the inside that counts
But isn't your personality
Just another way
To try to be pretty
Anyway?
And in the trying
Fail yourself

I am not fine
That all I want to do
Is sit down and watch football
And forget all of this
But I can't help but wonder
If football is just
Another means of oppression
Promising the athletic poor
Fame and money and other worthless things
Like college degrees
For the price of their spines
And their futures

I am not fine
That even sugar doesn't
Make me happy anymore
Because that is what I thought
I came to this planet for
And do I even want to stay?
But maybe it was never
For the sugar
Maybe all along
It was really
Just for you

EARTH

Prayer For Today

I'm sorry
For having gotten
So used to
Magic
That I forgot
To stop and
Marvel

BLOOM

I know.
I have always known.
Even as I married him,
That I was only on loan.
It couldn't be him
When
It has always been you.
I saw you in Ralph Hare-uh-mee-yo
as he chased me around the playground,
And in every beautiful brown boy since.
My heart called to you
Across worlds.
A sonar even as I slept,
Ping ping ping,
Searching.
It's true another woke me
To finish breaking my heart
So I could put it together
In the shape of you.
Your eyes are my home.
Dark
The richest soil.
The only place
I could possibly
Bloom.

I lie awake
And think of
Depleting
Money
Time
Youth
Then I close my eyes
And listen to the breath
Of my dog as he sleeps
And remember
Each day
I collect
So much more treasure
Than I will ever be able
To spend

TREASURE

Don't just fall in love with
Shoes and wine and lipstick and
Men.

<h1>DEAR WOMEN</h1>

Please, oh yes, and I am begging
As I ask this of you
I am on my knees for you, Women
Please fall in love with
The snorting sound you make when you laugh
And the weird hair that grows from your chin
And the delicious feeling of your flesh bouncing
As you jump and dance and shake that
Exquisite flat/big/small/round/jiggly/muscular booty of yours
Fall in love with your
Bare skin
Unadorned with false idols
With your off-key voice
And your crooked tooth
And that mole you always wished you didn't have
Love your thin/thick/gray/curly/straight/no hair
Please, I beg, fall in love with
Your hearts
Do not hate them when they break
And make a sound
Like a runaway train trying to stop
Screeching
It is their breaking
That makes them stronger, bigger
Able to hold unimaginable love
A love so great it can finally
Include yourself
That is how you claim your
Power
That is how you birth
A new world

HOME

The memory of
Our first kiss
Is not mine
The way the feeling of your heart
Beating in my fingertips is
The way the smell of your sweat
On white sheets is
It was not the tequila
No I did not forget
That kiss was home
And you don't remember home
It is a part of you
Felt only in its absence
How much longer
Must I wait to be
Home again

WEATHER

Like the lilac
You will sometimes not
Smell as sweet
Depending upon
The weather
You have endured
That year
Your leaves may be more sparse
And you may have fewer blossoms
But you will be
Just as beautiful
For continuing to bloom

It is no coincidence
That you cannot
Spell heart
Without hear
Your voice played
In the key
Of my soul
I know I could
Better breathe
If I were to
Hear it again
My heart misses it so

RESONANCE

There are still moments
When each fragment
Of my soul
Every shard
Of my body
All that I am
Aches
To be in your arms
And I wonder
How can I possibly
Live
Without you

Then I cry
Or I write
Or I dance
And suddenly
There is more of me
In this world
Then there was before
And I think
It must be
A good thing?

MORE

Tulips are what I like
I declared
Of the beautiful
Scentless and fragile cups
Carnations were too cheap
I knew
From watching how

         ROSES

They sold them at school
On Valentine's Day
To the boys inclined to buy them
For the kind of girls
That got flowers bought for them
While I watched in
Feigned ambivalence
(And secret despair)
So no, not carnations
Not gladiolas either
Which I thought were pretty
And told my mother so
"Those are funeral flowers" she said
Not to be loved, she didn't have to say
To her daughter who had never
Seen those flowers before
Or a funeral
But never roses in that first half of life
And often
Never flowers at all
My heart frozen from
Wanting emptily
For so many years

I don't care about flowers, I declared
To my husband, then my lover
They are a waste of money
Because they just die
(Like us)
And the little girl who picked
The purple flowers
Roots and all
Trailing dirt as she carried them
To her mother while her sister scoffed
"Those are weeds"
Crumbled a little and
Hid inside me
Behind my hardening heart

When I married my lover
At the wedding held for his mother
In the church for mine
I held the cousin to the tulips I wanted
Which my mother had insisted
Were not sturdy enough for a bouquet
(Or as it turned out
For a marriage)
The calla lilies were statuesque
And elegant
In the way I have never felt
Like the wedding dress I wanted
Tall and slim, simple and regal
For the body I didn't have
To wear in a life
That wasn't mine

Not that it wasn't lovely
The wedding
And those years with the man
Who tried to be my husband
But who was destined only
To be the bridegroom
Of hops and malt and water and yeast
So when I could no longer be
A tag-along in their life
I gathered my hardened heart
And the little girl with the purple weeds
Hiding behind it
And the teenager with the eyes of longing
Hidden behind cynical glasses
And we abandoned the
Stoic
Elegant
Scentless
Myth
Opening our hearts to what we
Had always found to be
So pedestrian
So common
So simple
Shattering the myth
That the rose was ever
Common
And that we ever had to be common either

Now
With the grace afforded to a woman
Who has lost and abandoned and found
Herself many times
A woman so fortunate
To be living my second or third
Or even fourth blooming
I honor the strength needed
To transform sunlight into life
To allow each delicate petal to be seen
To perfume the world with love
And to never apologize
For your thorns

CHOCOLATE

Sometimes when people say
That they don't like chocolate
I want to stop them
Put a hand on their arm
And whisper
"Oh dear, are you afraid to love?
It's scary, I know. But you must, dear."
Chocolate is
The food of the heart.

MY FAVORITE POET

My favorite poet
Is made from the clay found
Where the land meets the sea
His heart holds each leaf and feather
In the depths of its chambers
And because they know him as their own
The creatures trust him
With their words
Which he speaks
In a voice that sounds like an old truck
Driving down a dirt road
As lyrical as rain
And just as nourishing
Like all things true and beautiful
He makes me cry
And I am grateful
That every morning
He greets the sun as she rises
For he is the best of us
The best we have to offer her

There is a moth
In the backyard
With a broken wing
He is beautiful   THE MOTH
But he cannot fly
And I wonder what it means
Because I've seen enough
To know that
It doesn't mean nothing
Does he know it's over?
Is he making peace with his one brief life?
Or is he healing so he can fly again?
When I look tomorrow
He will be gone
Having disappeared into
A brighter future
Leaving me here
To ask myself
How much does my belief
About what happens to him
Matter

And in the end
You will save
No one   PIECES
By giving away
Pieces
Of yourself

Everything is meaningful
Until it's not
And the fires have made the sky
So strange
Like an eclipse
And I love to pour the hot water for my tea
From the electric kettle with the goose-neck
Into the mug I bought
Because it reminded me of
A him I once thought meaningful
Now I don't remember why
But the sky, oh the sky
With grays and pinks
Tones it never was
And will never be again
To watch it and
Hear the world turn the cicadas off
But someone forgot to tell
The air conditioner and the cars
To do the same
So they keep humming
While the cicadas and I
Watch the sky
Living the moment
As the ash of this
Not real world
Settles at my feet
Like a snow flurry
Witnessed by no one

SACRED

And god help me
I still want one of them
To come back and say
I was worth it
And mean it
But what of it?
He already has
And it changed nothing
Am I really so scared
To start anew
In this ash covered world
Where I start anew
Over and over
Scared? No
I am fearless now
That is true
Tired, though
I am tired of my stories
I will put them on the shelf
And trust that the person
Who comes for me
Will not need them
But will know me
By my ash covered heart

I am free now
And here are the dandelion seeds
Like quantum particles
And suddenly I remember the tea
And the mug
And the boy who I once thought
was everything
So I walk back the way I came
But nothing is quite the same
And I pick up stones
And think about keeping them
Making them sacred
Giving them meaning
But I put them back down again
Because when I let go
Everything is sacred

MOTHER

Thank your mother for me

For those beautiful eyes

That see the world as only you can

Thank your mother for me

For those hands that create

What never was before

Thank your mother for me

For that heart beating in your chest

The one that sounds like mine

Whispering love love love

Thank your mother for me

This dance of our soul
Is not about you
As handsome as you are
As much as I want to stroke your beautiful face
Kiss your lips of magic
Run my hands through the cool waterfall of you hair
A feeling tattooed on my heart
Like the butterfly on yours
This dance is about
Me.
Though you are a part, of course you are
The catalyst to my alchemy
The spark to my blaze
The raindrop that flowed down the mountain into
My ocean.
This dance is for
Me.

My love, you dance with me
Oh how you dance
And for that I bow down
But I am the goddess of this story
I am the keeper of this soul
This love is mine
It comes from me
It lives in me
It is
Me.

ME

And no one, my king
Not even you with your dark
chocolate eyes and
Your secret caramel heart
Your cheshire grin
Upon your buffalo face
Can take the piece of me
That I have found
Through loving you
Enough to love
Me.

Seeing god
Will stop you right in your tracks
The sun streaming
A heavenly beam
Through dark clouds
A honey bee shaking his
Little bee booty
As he dances with the lilac blossom
My dog's paws twitching
In his doggy daydreams
Where he endlessly chases squirrels
Seeing god
Will stop you right in your tracks
And if you get good at it
You can see god
Everywhere
Which makes it hard to
Press forward
When there is
Nowhere else to be

SEEING GOD

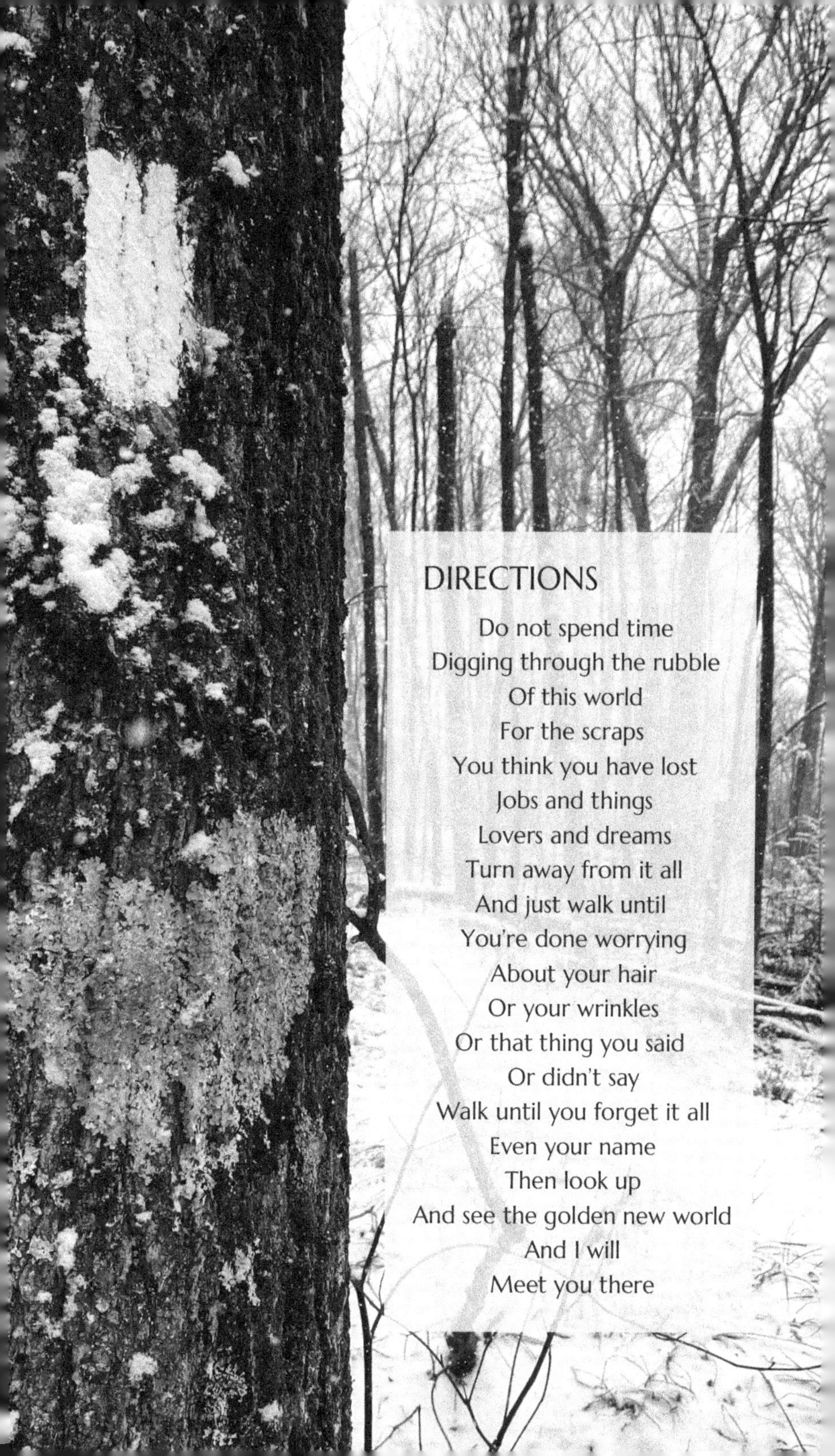

DIRECTIONS

Do not spend time
Digging through the rubble
Of this world
For the scraps
You think you have lost
Jobs and things
Lovers and dreams
Turn away from it all
And just walk until
You're done worrying
About your hair
Or your wrinkles
Or that thing you said
Or didn't say
Walk until you forget it all
Even your name
Then look up
And see the golden new world
And I will
Meet you there

PERENNIAL

May I remember that

I am not

An annual

Born to bloom once

After a short youth,

then die

May I remember

That I was made

To bloom

Again and again

and again

FIRE

Prayer For Today

May I remember that
Life and I are
Partners in this dance
And my soul will always
Lead
If I let it

I should have
I could have
I needed to
I can't believe I haven't
I must have missed my   TIME
Chance
Love
Moment
Hush child says my soul
You're right on time

ALONE

I am happy
Alone
I relish the time spent
With me
I make diligent study of
Self love
But once in a while
My heart aches
To feel
Your foot against
My foot

DEAR MEN

There are not two kinds of women
Ones broken loose to be used
Because they have been
Drunk or high or
Undressed
And then the good ones
Untouched in cardigans and pearls
If you have sullied one of us
You have sullied us all
We cannot be judged by our covers
Pain is written onto each of our pages
From what you have done
And what you've left undone
Of the sins of your fathers
All scars are ours
You cannot separate us
Into those worthy of your love
And those deserving your scorn
All have been tainted by your darkness
We are not two kinds
We are one
Woman

WHO I AM

If you think

That breaking my heart

Will make it stop

Loving you

Then you don't know

Who I am

PERFECT

You like to tell me
All the bad stuff
As if I don't know your flaws
Intimately
Maybe even more intimately
Than I know my own
Like you want to
Scare me away
But I am not afraid
Because anything that inspires me
To love
The way you do
Is perfect
Just as it is

HUNNY

Hunny

You called me

Not babe or sweetie

Hunny

What Pooh Bear adores

Because it is

Natural and

Sweet and

A little bit dangerous

To harvest

ANTICIPATION

Don't anticipate, you said
When I looked over my shoulder at you
Waiting
For the pain
For the growth
For the distance
Between us to finally
Close
For good.
How can I not?

When I said
That you are mine
As I choked
And bit you
I didn't mean
That I owned you
I meant that
You owned me

SUBMISSION

ENOUGH

I never said I would be easy

I said I love you

I said you are amazing

I said I see you, I know you,

I want you and

I hoped that was enough

My mind would like
To apologize
She has to do this a lot
For things that
Escape my lips
Born of fear
She says she was trying to
Protect me
But got it
Very wrong
My heart
Apologizes for nothing
She says she
Still loves you

SORRY

TRY

Please
I begged my soul
Release them from my heart
My soul whispered back
You cannot release them
They are a part of you
You have tried to
Stop loving them
You have tried to
Let them go
To forget and ignore
But have you tried
Loving them
More?

It's a shame
That we often see
Most clearly
Not through
The windshield
But from the
Rearview mirror

CLARITY

DEMANDS

My body demands

I worship her

This means

She will never

Let me

Let you

Touch her

Until you do

The same

I want you to
Fuck me lazily
On Sunday mornings
In a way that should be called
Making love
But we will call it
Fucking
Because we like to sound
A little bad
BAD

What is to become of me
I sometimes wonder
Of this woman
Whose life I am leading
Untethered

Do I continue to wander
Will I ever find a home
In the arms of the man
Who once was
The brown-eyed boy
I was supposed to love forever

Does he feel that?
Does he know?
Is he really just
Behind the curtain
Or is the curtain only hiding
An empty space
Where the next he
Hasn't arrived

Will it just be him
Until it's not
Will it ever just be me
And do I even want it to

Do I still write
With blind hope
That the words
That cannot change the past
Will somehow lead me
To my future
What is to become of me

UNTETHERED

Sometimes

The words fly all around

Above me

Like a flock of starlings

Full of magic

And omens

On those days

It is not my job

To catch them

And try to give them

Meaning

But to just watch them come

And let them go

WITNESS

THE CHILDREN

I try to remain
Positive
I don't fear
The world
But sometimes
A shriek
Rises up from my soul
Shattering my heart
When, God
Oh when
Will we finally protect
The children

MY HEART

My heart belongs
To someone else
I told him
And it's true
But the someone else
He's thinking of
Isn't really you
My heart belongs
To me now
Though it's been
A long time coming
She beats for me
And just for me
Does she do her
Lovely drumming

JOSÉ

How do I tell
The man at the
Donut shop
When he asks what
I do
That my work is in
Unseen realms
That I am a warrior
Of love
Sent here to help
Save us
With weapons of
Cookies and words and smiles
But maybe I underestimate
José

She asked me what I will do
When after all this time
I finally see you again
I told her that
I will take a deep breath
And feel my heart
I will look into your eyes
And memorize the line of your jaw
With my fingertips
I will inhale you
And honor myself
By remaining with my soul
In your presence
Because if there's one thing
I regret
It's the moments   **REMEMBER**
I forgot to
Remember everything

LEO

These days
I purr more than I roar
My claws are filed down
And I talk mostly of love
I am softer now
Worn with time
Polished with tears
No longer the feral woman
I once was
Docile even
But do not dare
Ever mistake me for
Tame

Call me not a lady
No lord rests in my bed
Call me not a queen
No crown lays on my head
Call me not a goddess
You'll find no temple mine
Simply call me Sun
And see how bright I shine

BRILLIANT

VICTORY

You asked me
What I wanted
And maybe I lied
When I didn't say
I want to make love to you
Every day
For the rest of our lives
And leave this world
Together
In victory for all the
Good we did
That seemed like too much
So I simply said I wanted
To be deeply loved
But aren't they really
Just the same

DELICATE

If you are hard
And hurting
And fearful
And have tried all you can
To change
The world
Outside
Take a deep breath
Look at the mirror
Inside
And begin
The delicate work
Of loving yourself

About the Author

Kerry Love is a writer and an artist. She was the little girl who used to write stories for fun and read books under her covers with a flashlight, long after bedtime.

Also by Kerry Love:
By Chance (with Jill Cammack)
Fine Tuning
Finer

kerrygretchenlove.com
@kerrygretchenlove

About the Images

- *Ippy-Oy-Ad* by Kathleen Spengler
- Cactus Heart and *Directions* by Chris Denu of VerticalRealmPhotography.com
- *Gravity, Forgive Me* by Jill Houston
- All other images by the author

She will sometimes shine bright

To show you the way

And sometimes go dark

To guide you with faith

Both in times full of hope

And on nights of despair

Just like my love

She will always be there

Goodnight Moon

www.ingramcontent.com/pod-product-compliance
Lightning Source LLC
Chambersburg PA
CBHW060332310726
48976CB00007B/2537